Anonymus

The Queen lace book

A historical and descriptive account of the hand-made antique laces of all

countries

Anonymus

The Queen lace book
A historical and descriptive account of the hand-made antique laces of all countries

ISBN/EAN: 9783742869029

Manufactured in Europe, USA, Canada, Australia, Japa

Cover: Foto ©Thomas Meinert / pixelio.de

Manufactured and distributed by brebook publishing software
(www.brebook.com)

Anonymus

The Queen lace book

THE

QUEEN LACE BOOK:

A

HISTORICAL AND DESCRIPTIVE ACCOUNT OF THE HAND-MADE

ANTIQUE LACES OF ALL COUNTRIES.

PART I.

MEDIÆVAL LACEWORK AND POINT LACE.

WITH

THIRTY ILLUSTRATIONS OF LACE SPECIMENS, AND SEVEN DIAGRAMS OF
LACE STITCHES.

LONDON:
"THE QUEEN" OFFICE, 346, STRAND, W.C.

1874.

PREFACE.

NTIQUE LACE has but recently again attracted the attention it so richly deserves, and which has been so lavishly bestowed on it by our forefathers. In the turmoil of the French Revolution the taste for the work of woman's skill and patience got lost, and the history of its manufacture became almost forgotten. When the interest for the old lace work revived, the geographical and chronological divisions, so well understood during the seventeenth and the greater part of the eighteenth century, were found nearly obliterated from the memory of the present generation, and had to be re-established. A written history of lace did not exist, and all information had to be gleaned from old wardrobe accounts, pattern books, and encyclopædias.

To Mrs. Bury Palliser belongs the merit of having first collected, with praiseworthy industry, documentary evidence about antique lace in her "History of Lace" (London: Sampson Low, Son, and Marston, 1869); and information about antique lace may be derived from the following books:

    S. Zedler.—Universal Lexicon. Leipzig, 1744.

    Ph. L. Savary.—Dictionnaire universel de Commerce. 1750.

    Roland de la Platière.—Encyclopèdie Méthodique.

    J. Peuchet.—Dictionnaire universel de la Géographie commercante. Paris, 1799.

    Accounts of the Keepers of the Great Wardrobe.—160 volumes, from I. Elizabeth 1558 to 1781. Now at the Audit Office.

    Pattern Books of the Sixteenth and Seventeenth Centuries.—A nearly complete list of them is given in Mrs. Palliser's "History of Lace."

Cavaliere Antonio Merli.—Origine ed uso delle Trine a filo di refe.
Genova, 1864 (privately printed). With 100 examples on
six lithograph plates.

Marquis d'Adda.—L'art et l'industrie aux XVI. et XVII. siècles.
Essai bibliographique sur les anciens modèles de lingeries,
de dentelles et de tapisseries, gravés et publiés aux XVI. et
XVII. siècles en Italie.

Signore Don Tommaso Torteroli.—Storia dei Merletti di Genova
lavorati in Albissola. Sinigaglia, 1863.

M. F. Aubry.—Rapport sur les Dentelles, les blondes, les tulles
et les broderies, fait à la Commission Française du Jury
Internationale de l'Exposition universelle de Londres, 1851.
Paris.

B. v. d. Dussen.—L'industrie Dentellière belge. Bruxelles, 1860.

The special object of this pamphlet is to **sift and** condense all available
information about antique lace, and to establish, with the aid of **a large**
collection of specimens, a systematical classification with regard to the origin
of hand-made lacework, the time and mode of its manufacture. Special
care has **been** taken that the engravings should show the characteristic
peculiarities of the work.

CONTENTS.

ILLUSTRATIONS.

FIRST DIVISION.—MEDIÆVAL LACEWORK.

SECOND DIVISION.—POINT LACE.

ILLUSTRATIONS—*continued.*

INTRODUCTION.

><><><

ACE, as a means of personal adornment, has for upwards of four centuries justly been in high favour with the fair sex; some notice therefore of the origin and history of this beautiful fabric, some account of its principal divisions with regard to workmanship, from a chronological and geographical point of view, cannot fail, by shewing the fortunate possessors of antique lace how, when, and where the various sorts have been made, and so indicating their true value, to interest English ladies.

ORIGIN OF LACE.

Embroidery of garments and vestments was universal in the Middle Ages. To obtain the desired effect gold, silver thread, and silk were applied to contrasting colours. Embroidery on solid linen was used for altar covers, grave clothes, &c.; but this being ineffective from a distance (unless worked with materials and colours which would not stand washing), perforating the linen by open-work embroidery, called Cutwork, suggested itself at an early period, and developed into Reticella proper during the fifteenth and sixteenth centuries. Contemporary with linen embroidery, and extensively practised, were Drawnwork and Darned Netting, in which all the old designs of embroidery, historical and Biblical groups, figures, emblems, and symbols could be imitated. Equally early was Knotted and Plaited Lacework, made either by unravelling the ends of the cloth, knotting or plaiting them in different designs, or more frequently by doing the same with loose threads, fastened and arranged on a pillow.

Linen Embroidery, Cutwork, Darned Netting, Drawnwork, Knotted and Plaited Laces were made in all convents during the Middle Ages, but exclusively for the use of the Church; and therefore they were little known to the lay world. Comparatively few specimens of the earliest work have been preserved: the revival of this mediæval Lacework for profane purposes begins about 1450.

In the second half of the sixteenth century, when art emancipated itself more or less from the Church, a desire was felt to make the costly embroidery movable, so that it could be worn on plain-coloured materials with the same effect as the old

fixed work, and could be changed from one garment to the other. For this purpose
Point Lace, which is but detached and movable embroidery, was introduced. At the
same time Knotted and Plaited work were improved to Pillow Lace proper, knotting
and plaiting being superseded by weaving.

Point and Pillow Lacework still remained confined to convents, Italy taking the
lead, and Spain following. The nuns taught it to their lay pupils, and the art of
producing it spread but slowly in the outside world from Italy to France, from Spain
to Flanders, Holland, and England.

During the sixteenth century Lace-making developed into a lay industry with
certain localities as centres for the manufacture of distinct kinds of Lace. The gradual
development of Lacework with regard to workmanship, style of design, and local
manufacture, suggests the following principal divisions :

A.—WITH REGARD TO WORKMANSHIP.

(1). *Mediæval Lacework.*—Linen Embroidery and Cutwork, Darned Netting,
Drawnwork, Reticella, Knotted work, Plaited work.

(2). *Point Lace.*

(3). *Pillow Lace.*

B.—WITH REGARD TO STYLE OF DESIGN.

1. Mediæval style up to 1550.
2. Geometrical style, 1550-1620.
3. Renaissance style, 1620-1720.
4. Rococo style, 1720-1770.
5. Dotted style, 1770-1810.

The design of Lace always followed the prevalent style of ornamentation of the
day, but the dates given as the limits of the different styles are to be understood with
a period of transition spreading over ten years before and after, when the character
of the design was a combination of the two styles. The characteristic features of the
five periods are very marked, and make it possible to decide with almost absolute
certainty on the time when a certain piece of Lace was made.

The *Mediæval style* introduces in the pattern symbolic groups, figures, and emblems,
monsters, sacred and other animals, trees, leaves, wreaths, and scrollwork.

The *Geometrical style* is a combination of squares, triangles, lozenges, wheels,
and segments of circles.

The *Renaissance style* is remarkable by fanciful flowing and undulating wreaths
and garlands of leaves, flowers, and scrollwork, first in close and compact patterns,

later more open, and connected with brides or buttonholed netground, the "jours" filled up with pointwork of endless variety. Point and Pillow Laces during this period were the most artistic in design, as well as the most elaborate in workmanship, and nearly every article of wear was trimmed with Lace.

With the *Rococo style* begins the period of decline in Lacework. **The graceful** patterns of the Renaissance are replaced by disconnected and stiff designs, rigid and angular bouquets and flowers meaninglessly crowded together.

In the *Dotted style* the design shrinks to small bouquets, intermixed with small fleurons, rosettes, tears (larmes), bees (mouches). **Drawn** muslin, and Blonde **supplant** the old Laces.

C.—WITH REGARD TO GEOGRAPHICAL CENTRES.

We remark that prior to 1550 Lace making was universal in **all the convents of Europe.** After 1550 **Venice takes the lead,** and holds its sway for more than a century in the manufacture of needle points, distributing patterns for imitation to its dependencies, to the Ionian Islands, to Spain, France, and the Netherlands. At the same time **Genoa enters the lists with knotted and plaited** laces, develops and spreads Lacemaking **on the pillow :** but the glories of **Venice** and Genoa pass away. During the second half **of the** seventeenth century France takes up the working **of** needle points ; the Netherlands get famous for their Pillow laces, until the French Revolution makes an end of all artistic and elaborate work, introduces flimsy Blonde, Drawn muslin, **and** revives the Braid or Tapework (lacette), held in scanty esteem in former times, and **called then** contemptuously "Point de canaille," or Beggars' lace.

FIRST DIVISION.

MEDIÆVAL LACEWORK.

CHAPTER I.

LINEN EMBROIDERY AND CUTWORK.

[OPUS SCISSUM (so called in the Wardrobe Accounts of Queen Elizabeth); PUNTO TAGLIATO (Italian); POINT COUPÉ (French).]

UTWORK was made by cutting out of the solid linen pieces in the shape of the intended openwork, and sewing over or button-holing the outlines left. The work was materially different from Reticella, as we shall show in its proper place. Coloured silks, gold, silver, and unbleached thread were used for working embroidery in relief.

Linen Embroidery and Cutwork were the favourite pastimes of nuns in all the mediæval convents of the globe, and were carried on under the guardianship of the Church until superseded, toward the middle of the sixteenth century, by Reticella proper, which still retained its old name (point coupé) for a long time. The linen used for the old Embroidery was all but imperishable—very different from the miserable fabric of the present day. Thus it happens that many specimens have been preserved, some of them dating as far back as the twelfth century, and showing all the strange vagaries of the styles and patterns of the different periods.

Specimens in pure mediæval style are met with, which were probably made for use in Gothic cathedrals. Later, during the fourteenth and fifteenth centuries, geometrical patterns were prevalent; and they gradually merged into the easier style of the Renaissance. (See illustration No. 2.) In the second half of the sixteenth century Linen embroidery and Cutwork were frequently worked in combination with Reticella, and specimens, admirable both in workmanship and design, are extant. (See illustration No. 1.) The south of Germany and Italy excelled in this kind of work; France and England seem to have been less skilful. In the cathedral of Prague an altar cloth of Embroidery and Cutwork is preserved, worked by Ann of Bohemia, queen of Richard II.; a portion of it is exhibited at the South Kensington Museum.

[*Plate 1.*

FIG. 1. LINEN EMBROIDERY, CUTWORK, AND RETICELLA. (Late Sixteenth Century.)

FIG. 2. LINEN EMBROIDERY AND CUTWORK. (Sixteenth Century.—Geometrical Style.)

CHAPTER II.

DARNED NETTING.

[OPUS ARANEUM; SPIDERWORK; POINT CONTÉ (French); LACIS; PUNTA A MAGLIA QUADRA, PUNTA A STUORA (Italian); PUNTAS DE RANDAS (Spanish); GUIPURE D'ART, FILET BRODÉ À REPRISES (Modern).]

DARNED NETTING dates as far back as Linen Embroidery; it was extensively practised during the Middle Ages, and very probably much earlier. Soon after the invention of wood block printing, a great number of pattern books for this kind of work appeared in Germany, Italy, and France; in fact, all the pattern books up to 1550 are well nigh exclusively devoted to Darned Netting.

The designs reproduced in these books were taken from the relics of Gothic and eastern architecture, from ancient embroideries and mediæval goldsmith work.

Darned Netting was worked on drawn, knotted, and twisted net, with gold, silver, silk, flax, thread and fibre, both in plain and varied colours. The flat pattern was done in real darning or "au passé," not in cross stitch, as used in the worsted work of a later period; the outline and prominent parts were sometimes thrown into relief with a thicker thread.

The earlier specimens for ecclesiastical ornamentation and in pure mediæval style, reproduce the lozenge and gammadion pattern, fleur de lys, the Gothic monsters (see illustration No.), and graceful foliage of the Middle Ages (see illustration No.), in combination with scriptural subjects and groups sacred and profane.

Darned Netting, prior to the sixteenth century, was principally used for borders of altar covers and grave clothes, the flat being ornamented with alternating squares of lacis and plain linen.

After 1500 a few traces of the geometrical style of design appear: but Darned Netting, though often found in connection with the Reticella of the period, always preserves the mediæval character of design.

During the seventeenth century, when Darned Netting was employed for the ornamentation of table covers, bed curtains, and coverlets, armorial shields, coronets, monograms, conventional flowers and bouquets, animals and figures of a profane character are introduced into the pattern; but mediæval designs, as given in the earlier sampler books, are still predominant.

To fix the country where a specimen of Darned Netting has been made is difficult, the pattern books spreading this kind of work uniformly and rapidly all over Europe.

The use of silver, gold, silk, unbleached thread, or fibre, points to the Latin races—Italy, Spain, and France, with their preference for bright and contrasting colours. Plain flax thread indicates the sober taste of the North of Germany and England.

Specimens bearing the date of their working are scarce ; and the test of style in design can hardly be applied to this kind of work after 1500, the same pattern books being used for centuries after.

An interesting passage about darned netting in England occurs in Canon Rock's book on "Textile Fabrics in the South Kensington Museum," which we quote :

"By our English women, hundreds of years gone by, amongst other applications of the needle one was to darn upon linen netting, or work thereon with other kinds of stitchery, religious subjects for church use, or flowers and animals for household furniture.

"In this country such a sort of embroidery was called net-work—filatorium—as we learn from the Exeter Inventory, where we read that the cathedral possessed, A.D. 1327, three pieces of it for the use of the altar."

Darned Netting in England, as practised during the seventeenth century, has a style of its own, by introducing into the pattern wheels and lozenges, copied from the contemporary Pillow Laces of Genoa.

Of this style of work the modern Darned Netting, called "guipure d'art," is a revival; and it certainly could be vastly improved if the graceful floral patterns of mediæval origin were copied.

[*Plate 2.*

FIG. 3. DARNED NETTING ON KNOTTED NET (Mediæval Style).

FIG. 4. DARNED NETTING ON TWISTED NET (Mediæval Style).

CHAPTER III.

DRAWNWORK. *

[OPUS TIRATUM ; PUNTO TIRATO (Italian).]

RAWNWORK ranks equal in antiquity with Cutwork and Darned Netting; it can be traced back to the twelfth century in altar covers and winding sheets that are still preserved.

The earliest specimens were made by drawing part of the horizontal and vertical threads of a piece of linen or silk, keeping the pattern intact, and forming the remaining threads—generally groups of three—into a square network by

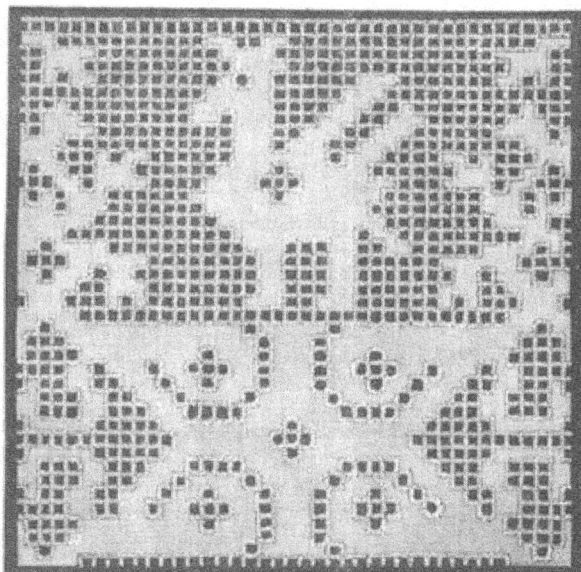

FIG. 5. DRAWN WORK (Mediæval Style—German).

overcasting them either with a separate thread of the same, or with one of a different colour. The ground of the pattern was either perforated with Cutwork or embroidered. (See illustration No. 5.)

c 2

The mediæval designs, although of necessity stiffer and less varied, resemble closely those used for Darned Netting of the same period. Specimens are comparatively scarce, very probably because Darned Netting was much easier to work, and proved more effective.

After 1550, when geometrical patterns were the prevalent fashion, Drawnwork adapted itself but poorly to the style of the period. More artistic taste is shown in Drawnwork—in imitation of Reticella—which was made towards 1600. Horizontal bands of different widths were drawn, and the vertical threads joined and overcast to form the pattern. (See illustration No. 7.)

The Renaissance period brought about a still more decided improvement in this kind of Lacework. Groups, figures, armorial shields, heraldic devices, foliage, arabesques, and scrolls were worked out in pleasing contrast by overcasting the threads forming the net with coloured floss silks. (See illustration No. 6.) Drawnwork of this description seems to have been worked to the highest perfection in Italy during the seventeenth century—specimens of an earlier date are rare, and less artistic in design ; it was used for ornamental insertions and borderings. Scarce known in England until very recently, it certainly deserves revival, considering the artistic taste of the designs, its utility for decorative purposes, and the comparative simplicity of its execution.

Drawnwork of any kind, however, could not compete with the sumptuous Points and elaborate Pillow laces of the Renaissance and early Rococo period (1620-1750). The art of producing it lingered on, and was all but forgotten, when, with the decline of Lacemaking and the introduction of narrow Mechlin and Valenciennes Laces in dotted style, a sudden revival took place. German, French, and English ladies began to imitate the old Point and Pillow Laces in drawn and embroidered muslin, and the easy informal fashion in dress was favourable to the development of this kind of needlework.

The pattern, ground, and stitches of antique Lace were copied by drawing, dividing, and reuniting the fine muslin threads ; the raised parts were reproduced by embroidered flowers, corded outlines, and sometimes by patchwork.

Specimens of beautiful design and workmanship, done in this manner, closely resembling real Lace, are yet to be met with.

Germany, and especially Denmark, excelled in this kind of needlework, which was known under the names of *Dresden Point, Hamburg Point, Tonder Lace.* In England it was called *Indian Work* ; in France, *Broderie de Nancy.*

At the present day Drawnwork is made in Portugal after the fashion of Fig. 7, and in Brazil in imitation of Fig. 5. It is a curious fact, that many traces of old Lacework are still to be found in countries formerly under Portuguese rule or influence. Like the Phœnicians in ancient times, the Portuguese traders and missionaries introduced European manufactures wherever they established their settlements, in the interior of Africa and in South America. The beautiful Embroidery and Drawnwork, made at the Philippine Islands with the fibre of Chinagrass (*Bœhmeria nivea*), is well known.

[*Plate 3.*

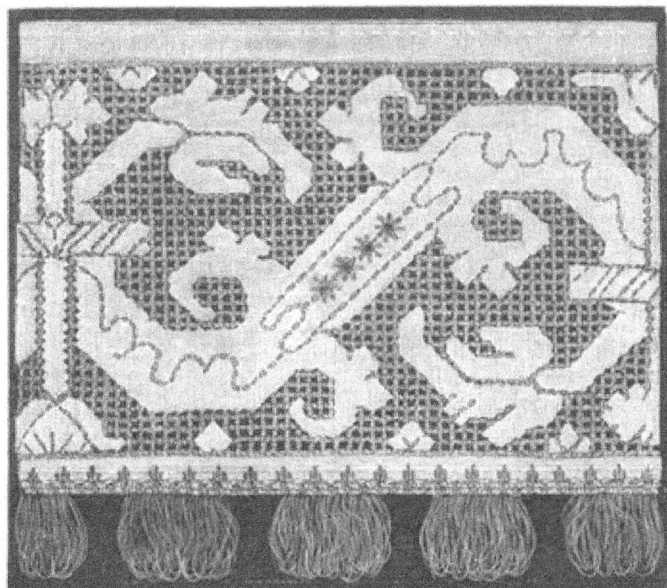

FIG. 6. DRAWN WORK (Renaissance Style, Red Floss Silk on Linen—Italian).

FIG. 7. DRAWN WORK (Late Geometrical Period—Italian).

CHAPTER IV.

RETICELLA.

[GREEK LACE; PUNTO A RETICELLA; PUNTO D'AERE (Italian).]

RETICELLA and Cutwork are often mistaken for each other, although they are very different in the working. Cutwork was produced by cutting the pattern out of the solid linen, and rope-stitching or overcasting the outlines left; in Reticella the leading lines of the design were formed by drawing threads, but more generally by arranging and fixing groups of threads in a linen or plaited thread frame, the latter firmly tacked down to a piece of parchment. Diagonal and intersecting lines were thrown across with the needle, the crossings secured, and then all the foundation threads either covered with an evenly twisted thread (rope work), or worked over with the buttonhole and Genoa stitch. (See Figs. *a, b, c, d*.)

Fig. *a*. Buttonhole Stitch.

Fig. *b*. Rope Stitch.

Fig. *c*. On Three Threads. GENOA STITCH.

Fig. *d*. On Two Threads.

The enlargement of the foundation pattern into decorative designs was effected by adding row upon row of buttonhole or Genoa stitch, and the work was finished by ornamenting the outlines with projecting points or knobs called thorns or picots. The materials used for Reticella work were flax thread and silk, both in plain and varied colours.

Reticella, although mentioned in the Sforza Inventory 1493, essentially belongs to the sixteenth century, and only a very few specimens can be traced back to an earlier date. The first pattern book for this kind of work (Federico Vinciolo) appeared 1587 in Paris, and seems to be a collection of designs used in Italy for fifty years previous to this date. Vinciolo's book, which likewise contained patterns for Darned Netting and Drawn-work, was republished in various French editions between 1587 and 1623, and was reprinted, copied, translated, and pirated in Italy, Switzerland, Germany, Flanders, and England.

It is now very scarce; a complete edition, in five parts, was sold last year in London for £45.

The designs of Reticella are of endless variety; and although somewhat stiff and formal, they are generally very tastefully arranged and of artistic effect.

The purely geometrical patterns in simple outline work may be considered as the oldest; later, segments of circles and triangles in solid work were added, and wheelwork introduced; until, towards the end of the sixteenth century, Reticella loses more and more its geometrical character, and adapts itself, as far as the peculiarities of the work will permit, to the style of the Renaissance period, and so merges gradually into real Point lace.

Reticella, under the teaching of Venice, was principally worked in the Ionian Islands, and recognised as Greek lace; it was likewise produced in all the convents of the leading Italian towns. The specimens from Zante, Corfu, &c. (see illustration No. 9), show reminiscences of Eastern origin in their design. Naples, Rome, Florence, and Milan produced Reticella patterns in a style more or less of their own.

In Germany, France, Spain, and Flanders, Reticella was made only to a very limited extent; it was merely an imitation of the Italian patterns spread by Vinciolo's and other pattern books; it has therefore become difficult to identify the special work of these countries. English Reticella is easily distinguished by its quaint combination of different styles, patterns, and stitches: elaborate samplers (Samcloths), called Elizabethan, of English Reticella work, are extant, and should be carefully preserved.

Reticella was the favourite Lace with the royal ladies of the house of Medicis, both in Italy and France; the Spanish court under Philip II., as well as the English nobles under Elizabeth, likewise adopted the fashion. The ruffs and manchettes of the period were made of the finest Reticella in combination with Cutwork and Drawnwork. Of these finer Laces but little remains—they perished under the rotting influence of starch and wear; only the coarser fabric, used for borderings of altar covers and shrouds, is known to the present generation, under the name of Greek or furniture lace. The style and patterns of these laces are too familiar to require illustration.

The bridal and carnival Laces (see illustrations 8 and 10) much in fashion at the beginning of the seventeenth century, deserve special notice; they formed an important feature in the trousseaux of Italian ladies, and were worn by the bride on her wedding day, as well as during the festivities, masquerades, &c., that followed the marriage; they had the crest or devices of both bride and bridegroom introduced into the pattern. In contemporary portraits these, as well as Reticella Laces of earlier date, are copied to the minutest detail, and much information as to design and workmanship can be gleaned from these sources.

Early in the seventeenth century the Points of the Renaissance period superseded Reticella as Dress Lace; but the production of the latter never ceased either in the Ionian Islands or in Malta until late in the eighteenth century; there it was used for the ornamentation of altar covers, grave cloths, and household furniture. The curiosity hunters unearthed this kind of Lacework (almost forgotten) when railroads and steamboats opened for research localities until then well nigh inaccessible. Quantities of the coarse so-called Greek lace have since appeared in the market; it is, however, but little

Plate 4.

FIG. 8. BRIDAL LACE, with the devices of the families "Dello Rovere " and "D'Urbino.
(Late Geometrical Period—Italian.)

FIG. 9. RETICELLA, from Corfu.

appreciated, and are contemptuously styled furniture Lace, although well preserved specimens are most effective for dress purposes, and are far more decorative from an artistic point of view than the flimsy fabrics of the present day.

Fig. 10   CARNIVAL LACE (late Sixteenth Century—Italian).

Reticella has not escaped revival in this age of imitation ; but, unfortunately, the least artistic patterns of coarse workmanship have been selected for reproduction—and, strange to say, these very indifferently worked copies are offered at higher prices than those for which the original work can be bought.

CHAPTER V.

KNOTTED LACE.

[PUNTO À GROPO or GROPARI ; MACRAMÉ (Italian) ; GEKNÜPFTE SPITZEN (German).]

NOTTED BORDERS occur on robes and garments of the Byzantine period, and seem to have been in use amongst Eastern nations even at an earlier date. A fringe of loose threads was formed at the end of the material—linen, silk, gold, or silver tissue—by drawing the warp threads, and then binding or knotting the weft threads together in tassels. The more artistic development of knotting in elaborate designs commences with the general revival of mediæval Lacework during the second half of the fifteenth century. This kind of Lacework is first mentioned in the Sforza Inventory (1493), and patterns are given in the pattern books of Taglienti and Il Specchio, between 1530 and 1550. The knotting was then done in separate stripes by fixing leading horizontal threads on a heavy pillow filled with sand, and fastening to them vertical threads for working. But knotting seems never to have been extensively practised. Specimens are scarce, and only found in Italy, where *punto à gropo* flourished during the geometrical period, 1550 to 1620, with the Romagna, Genoa, Naples, Sicily, and the Ionian Islands as centres ; this knotted work did not enjoy any great popularity in Italy is further proved by the rare occurrence of working patterns in the sample books of the period.

The mode of working made knotted Lace a heavy and somewhat coarse fabric, only fit for borderings of church and household linen, curtains, and scarfs, not for dress ; on the introduction of the pillow, which doubtless originated with this kind of Lace, easier and more effective methods of producing dress Laces by plaiting and weaving were soon discovered, and consequently knotting neglected or altogether abandoned. Knotted Lace, however, was made all through the sixteenth century, but it could not hold its own either with Reticella or the plaited work of Genoa. It was a curiosity then as it is now, confined to Italy, and did not take part in the pilgrimage of lace-making to France and the Netherlands after 1600. At what time this Lace was named Macramé—a word of Arabic origin, meaning a fringed border—is not known.

Two kinds of Macramé are met with—the one tightly knotted throughout, and partly raised in rims or ridges (see illustration No. 12) ; the other worked flat, part of the design being in loose knots (see illustration No. 11), with picots and buttonhole stitch introduced. The patterns bear mostly the stamp of the geometrical period ; in rare cases an attempt is made to reproduce more complicated designs, such as beetles, lobsters, spiders, &c. (See illustration No. 12.)

During the Renaissance period, and long afterwards, no trace of Macramé work can be found. The fringes to the national headdress and scarf of Southern Italy were allowed to float freely again as loose threads or tassels.

Plate 5.

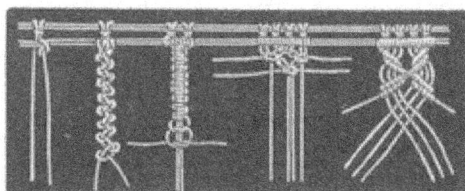

Figs.

a   b   c   d   e

KNOTS FOR MACRAMÉ LACE.

FIG. 11. MACRAMÉ (Geometrical Style—Italian).

During the present century (1843) the art of knotting Macramé in ornamental designs has been revived by the exertions of the Baroness d'Asti at the Albergo del Poveri in Genoa, and has spread from there to the villages along the Riviera.

Macramé is made on a heavy pillow. To a leading thread fastened horizontally, doubled threads of equal length are looped, so as to form a deep fringe. The working threads must be about four times as long as the width intended. When a sufficient length of fringe to commence with is thus prepared, another horizontal thread is fastened to the cushion with a pin, and held firmly with the right hand across and over the vertical threads, whilst the left hand loops each of the latter in a single knot, or twice over in a buttonhole knot, thus forming the horizontal cord-like rows of the footing.

Fig. 12. Macramé (Late Sixteenth Century—Italian).

Patterns are worked in the same way, using right and left hands, holding one of the vertical threads in the required slope with either hand, and working the others over it. If it is not desired that the ends of the threads should form a fringe, they may be gradually worked in by buttonhole stitch at the sides of the scallops, and be then at intervals thrown out and cut off two or three at a time.

An attempt to describe the working of Macramé more minutely is practically useless; the intricacies of the handling cannot be put into words. A scrap of the old work and the diagrams given are far more efficient teachers.

CHAPTER VI.

PLAITED LACE.

[Genoa Point; Merletti di Genoa (Italian); Point Génois (French);
Geflochtene Spitzen (German).]

WITH the introduction of the pillow for Knotted Laces, plaiting suggested itself, and was found a much easier work, more suitable for a greater variety of patterns, and for the production of the much coveted insertions, vandyked and scalloped borders, in a lighter style than could be obtained by knotting or in Reticella. Plaited Laces soon, therefore, became the favourite work on the pillow; bobbins were introduced to prevent the entanglement of the loose threads, and pins were used to fix and vary the design.

The earlier patterns are copied from Reticella in all its varieties and in the same materials — white and unbleached flax-thread and coloured silks, but more especially in gold and silver thread. Originated in Italy towards the close of the sixteenth century, and developed in Genoa, the plaited work was taken up by all the lace workers of Continental Europe. It was applied to trim the robes of courtiers and ecclesiastics; to ornament the uniforms and scarfs of the soldiery, to border banners, altar frontals, and even table covers and bedhangings.

Many of the pattern books of the period contain instructions and designs for plaiting in gold and silver thread. Lucca, Genoa, Florence, Venice, and Milan were noted for gold and silver plaiting; and Spain's early speciality in plaited Lacework of this kind as well as in coloured silks, called "Point d'Espagne," is well authenticated. All through the seventeenth century Spain supplied the Courts of Europe with these wire Laces; and up to the present time much gold, silver, and tinsel Lace is made for church purposes at Barcelona, Valencia, and Seville. Some fine specimens in revival and imitation of the old style were to be seen at the last Paris Exhibition. France under Colbert manufactured "Point d'Espagne" of inferior material and workmanship; so did Germany, Flanders, and England at the same period. In the South Kensington Museum a scarf given by James V. to one of his retainers about 1533 is preserved; it is richly embroidered on silk, and bordered with pointed scallops of gold wire plaited in geometrical designs. But most of the real gold and silver laces have perished in the melting pot, whilst those made of base metal and tinsel were thrown away when tarnished by time and wear.

Considering the uniformity in design, and the very limited ingenuity displayed in the manufacture of these wire Laces, they have but little interest for the Lace student. We turn, therefore, to the plaited fabric in linen thread which takes such a prominent place amongst Dress Laces during the sway of the ruff, and which was held in still higher estimation when the falling collar came into fashion. It was Genoa again (with its

Plate 6.

Fig. 13. PLAITED LACE, POINT DE GÊNES FRISÉ (late Sixteenth Century).

dependencies along the Riviera), who towards 1600 emancipated herself **from** the purely geometrical designs of Reticella proper, and, by adopting the **lozenge** pattern, produced the vandyked and scalloped border Laces (Point de Gênes **Frisé**, illustration Fig. **13**).

Albissola, **a** village on the road from Savona to Genoa, was famous during **the** sixteenth century for its Plaited Laces in black and white thread, in silk of different colours, and in aloe fibre, and at **a** later period rivalled even with Genoa in the manufacture of fine Pillow Guipures. The manufacture seems to have been of sufficient importance to furnish the materials for a special history of this fabric, written by Tommaso Torteroli, of Savona, and published at Sinigaglia, 1863.

Pointed patterns of the Genoese fabrics, plaited throughout, were much used as edgings to ruffs, collarettes, and cuffs before 1600. When the ruff was discarded for the falling collar early in the seventeenth century a heavier Lace was found necessary. Lozenges and outlines in Genoa stitch (still in combination with plaited work, and later **with** woven parts) gave the required weight, and for many decades Genoa provided the **world** of fashion with the characteristic scallops (Fig. 14) so faithfully depicted in the portraits of the period.

Point de Gênes Frisé continued **to be worn as the dress Lace** *par excellence* until about 1660, when the flowing **wig introduced by Louis XIV.** gave a final blow to the falling collar, the pride **of Charles I. and his cavaliers.** Long curls, covering the shoulders, were inconsistent **with Genoa collars; and in Charles** II.'s time the latter shrank to the **Lace** cravat made **of needle-point. The reign of** mediæval Lacework was at an end, **and** gave way to **more elaborate productions of** needle and pillow, initiated by the Renaissance period.

The modern imitations of these Plaited Laces were first made in Malta, introduced there by Lady Hamilton Chichester in 1833; now they are manufactured in enormous quantities in the Auvergne (Le Puy), and in Buckinghamshire, and have become, under the names of Maltese, Cluny, and Yak Lace, the most important article of the Lace trade.

CHAPTER VII.

TAPE AND BRAID LACES.

[Tænia poynt; Beggar's Lace; Mezzo punto (Italian); Point de Lint; Point de Canaille; Lacet (French).]

EFORE we take leave of Plaited Laces, we must mention the Braid and Tape Guipures: These were first started in Italy as cheap imitations of the former, and were produced in all shapes, materials, and designs. This work adapted itself to every style; it never died out, and dragged its existence through all the centuries of Lacework up to the present day. There is hardly any heavy Point or Pillow Lace, which has not been counterfeited in Tape or Braid work. The early productions of this kind were not without merit in design and workmanship. Braid or Tape was carefully woven on the pillow, in rare cases worked in Genoa stitch or plaited, the open spaces being filled up with bars, called brides or legs, and later with meshwork.

A favourite pattern of Tape Laces of the sixteenth century is a heavy conventional scrollwork, repeated in oblong partitions, with solid footings and sidings. The tape used is generally plain and solid, differing in width every here and there, but in the more artistic specimens whimsically perforated, part lightly, part loosely woven. Crossings and doublings of the braid or tape gatherings and puckerings at sharp corners are entirely avoided in the old work of the finer kind, and the bends carefully adjusted without folds; the workmanship is altogether superior to the lacet work of the present day. The lines of the pattern in the earlier specimens of the sixteenth and seventeenth century are connected by simple brides, twisted in two bars, rarely ornamented with projected loops; after 1700 pillow-woven network was used for this purpose, and the fillings executed with a very limited number of point stitches. The chief beauty of this old braidwork consists in the easy flowing design, the graceful adjustment of the brides, and the judicious choice of the point stitches for fillings. The Laceworkers of the present day revel in torturing their braid by doubling and crossing it into meaningless and angular patterns, connecting the lines of the design with rigid and stiff bars, and filling every nook and corner with a distressing variety of point stitches; they forget, that simplicity and taste are the first requirements for artistic work.

Plate 7.

Fig. 14. COLLAR LACE made at Genoa about 1640.

SECOND DIVISION.

POINT LACE.

OINT LACE proper took its origin from Reticella, and must be considered as the perfection of Lacework so far as regards artistic design and ingenious workmanship. Entirely wrought with the needle, and employing only one stitch—the buttonhole stitch, tight or loose—Point Lace displays a fertility of invention, and an amount of woman's patience, marvellous to contemplate. The minuteness of the work, and the variety of microscopic forms and devices are so astonishing, that the student of antique Lace turns with disgust from the presumption of modern braiders, who call their miserable work by the old name. Years, nay a lifetime, eyesight, and health, have been spent upon finishing many a piece of Point Lace, which, to turn out in trumpery imitation, would take only a few days of a modern Lace-worker's time. It is therefore sad to observe how even the appreciation of Old Point is lost amongst the ladies of the present generation, and only remains as an attribute of the high-born and well-bred. Glittering gewgaws and tawdry productions of the machine loom are preferred before the delicate fabric of woman's real art and skill; whilst in the seventeenth century, when a feeling for true art and a cultivated taste pervaded all classes, fortunes were spent in Point Lace, and the costly treasure was left as an heirloom to generations to come.

Even Ruskin, the great art critic, has quite recently (in a letter addressed to the Duke of St. Albans, and read by him at the distribution of prizes to students of the Night Art Class, connected with the Mechanics' Institute at Mansfield) raised his voice for the revival of antique artistic Lacework, and has pointed out most forcibly the value of the same, compared with the poor substitutes of the machine loom, and, we may add, of modern fancy work. He says: "There is still some distinction between Machine-made and Hand-made Lace. I will suppose that distinction so far done away with, that, a pattern once invented, you can spin Lace as fast as they now do thread. Everybody then might wear not only Lace collars, but Lace gowns. Do you think that, when everybody could wear them, everybody would be proud of wearing them? A spider may perhaps be rationally proud of his own cobweb, even though all the fields in the morning are covered with the like, for he made it himself; but suppose a machine spun it for him? Suppose all the gossamer were Nottingham made? If you think of it, you will find the whole value of Lace as a possession depends on the fact of its having a *beauty* which has been the reward of industry and attention. That the thing is itself a price—a thing everybody cannot have. That it proves, by the look of it, the ability of the maker; that it proves, by the rarity of it, the dignity of its wearer—either that she has been so industrious as to save money, which can buy, say, a piece of jewellery, of gold tissue, or of fine Lace—or else that she is a noble person, to whom her neighbours concede as an honour the privilege of wearing finer dress than they. If they all choose to have Lace too—if it ceases to be a price, it becomes, does it not, only a cobweb? The real good of a piece of Lace, then, you will find, is that it should show first, that the designer of it had a pretty fancy; next, that the maker of it had fine fingers; lastly, that the wearer of it has worthiness or dignity enough to obtain what is difficult to obtain, and common sense enough not to wear it on all occasions."

We strictly limit the designation of Point proper to Lace, entirely made with the needle on a parchment pattern, although the term is frequently misapplied to Pillow Laces, as Genoa Point, Mechlin Point, Point de Paris, Honiton Point, &c.

As a general rule how to distinguish Point Lace from Pillow Lace, it may be considered, that any Lace (besides Reticella), in which button-hole stitch occurs, falls under the category of Point proper.

The following technical terms are used in connection with Point Lace: The solid part of the Lacework as a whole is called *Pattern*; either worked level, *Flat Point*; or partly raised, *Raised Point*. The intervening spaces are either left open, or connected by irregular threads; the latter overcast with button-hole stitch (*brides claires*), or variously ornamented with picots (*brides ornés*), and called *ties* in England, *brides* in France, *legs* in Italy. Sometimes the open spaces are filled up with meshwork. For the former kind we shall adopt the French term "*Point Guipure à bride,*" or Guipure *par excellence*; the correct name for the latter is "*Point Guipure à Réseau,*" or Grounded Point. The raised and generally buttonholed rim, forming the outline of the pattern, is called *Cordonet*; the open work and fancy stitches are termed *Fillings, Jours*, or *Modes*. The little loops, knots, or knobs ornamenting the Cordonet are called *Pearls, Thorns,* or *Picots*. *Footing* or *engrêlure* is the narrow stripe of Lace sewn to the upper edge, by which the body of the Lace is fastened to the dress.

The way in which Old Point (Spanish and Italian) was worked can be seen in partly finished pieces, still fastened to the parchment pattern, and exhibited at the South Kensington Museum.

The general outline of the pattern was first designed or traced on a white or green parchment, and the fancy stitches roughly sketched in. The parchment was then tacked firmly to coarse linen folded double, and the outline of the design finally marked out by guiding a strand of two or more threads along the tracery, and well securing it by small stitches at equal intervals of from ⅛in. to ¼in. in length. The holes into which the stitches were fastened were pricked through the mounted parchment before placing and securing the outline threads. By overcasting the latter with buttonhole stitches the Cordonet was formed, and appeared more or less raised, according to the number and thickness of the underlying threads. Between and parallel to the Cordonet outlines the Pointwork with its fancy stitches and perforations was worked in. Brides or net ground were put in sometimes before buttonholing the outlines, and sometimes after. The second tier of raised work, and the **centres with their ornamental loops** and picots, had to be worked separately and sewn to **the Cordonet.** By **passing a** sharp knife between the folds of the underlying linen, **the loops that secured the** Work were cut, and the finished Lace came off the parchment.

Spanish, Venetian, and early Point de France were worked in large oblong pieces or stripes, joinings being avoided as much as possible. The Grounded Points of Alençon, Argentan, and Brussels, were executed in small pieces **or** sections by different hands, on the principle of divided labour, and were joined afterwards.

Point Lace **proper** was not produced to any extent **before** 1620, **whatever** may be **said to** the **contrary.** Reticella work of the seventeenth century **is** the nearest approach to it ; but **still** retains **traces** of plaiting and Genoa stitch, which were never employed in real Point. **It** took a long time to transplant Point Coupé, and especially the Genoese Lozenge Laces (Point de Genês), so much in fashion under Louis XIII. *Point proper* became the dress Lace *par excellence* under Louis XIV.

The manufacture of Point Lace can be traced to distinct centres in Italy, Spain, France, and Belgium, whilst in Germany, Denmark, Sweden, and England, Point seems to have been the isolated handiwork of individuals. The Lace produced within the influence of these centres differs more or less in design and details of workmanship ; geographical and local subdivisions therefore afford the readiest method whereby to refer a piece of Point Lace to the country, and even to the locality, of its origin. The style of design supplies the required indications as to the time *when* the Lace was made. Here it may be observed, that *where* a piece of Lace was *bought* gives no clue whatever to its real origin, because valuable Lace travels all over the world, backwards and forwards, like gold, silver, and precious stones.

The following cities may be considered as authenticated principal centres for Point Lace manufacture during the seventeenth and eighteenth centuries :

> Italy.—Venice.
> Spain.—Castille (Escorial).
> France.—Lonray, Alençon, and Argentan.
> Belgium.—Brussels.

The minor and branch establishments for Needle-made Lace we shall mention as we proceed with the description of the different fabrics.

CHAPTER VIII.

VENICE POINT.

PUNTO DI VENEZIA.   POINT DE VENISE.

ENICE originated *Point proper*, and produced it in infinite variety of design
and workmanship. Point may have been worked there in isolated instances
before 1600, but it came prominently forward towards the middle of the
seventeenth century. Designs given in the pattern books of the sixteenth
century are all of the Reticella type, and cannot be brought under the
designation of real Point. This applies to the often quoted Lace collar, "Scolpito in
basso relievo," on which the Florentine poet, Firenzuola, composed an elegy between
1520 and 1530. The Points mentioned in the Italian patternbooks of the sixteenth
century, as Punti Gasii, Trezola, Rimessi, Lavori, Bavari, Frisi, Fiamenghi, Incrociati,
Di Picciole, Opere à Mazzette, &c., seem to refer to the various stitches in which the
details of Reticella were executed. In the present day all elaborate Point work is indis-
criminately ascribed to Venice, and the parental claims of Spain and France to many
of the finest productions are entirely disregarded.

A careful scrutiny of many hundred specimens with regard to their origin, in
connection with the testimony of pattern books and contemporary writers on the subject,
have led us to the following result as to the distinguishing characteristics of Venice-made
Point. In Venice Point Guipure—flat or raised—the pattern is always connected by an
irregular *network* of pearled brides. Real brides connecting the flowers here and there
hardly ever occur; and the number of picots attached to one single branch of the brided
network never exceeds two. The elaborately-ornamented detached brides and a multi-
plicity of picots are characteristic of Spanish Point and early Point de France.

Two subdivisions of Venetian Pointwork, besides those described as Mediæval
Lacework in the First Division, have been established by Cavaliere Merli in his pamphlet
" Origine ed uso delle Trine a filo di refe."

A. *Punto Tagliato a Fogliami* (Raised Point).

B. *Punto in Aria* (Flat Point).

Plate 8.

FIG. 15. VENETIAN GROUNDED POINT (Rococo Style).

FIG. 16. VENETIAN RAISED POINT IN YELLOW SILK (Renaissance Style).

SUBDIVISION A.

PUNTO TAGLIATO A FOGLIAMI.

(PUNTO A RELIEVO, PUNTO TUTTO PER FILO, PUNTO A FILO GRANO CON MEZZO-RELIEVO, GROS POINT DE VENISE, ROSE POINT).

The design of this Point represents a scrollwork of flowers, stalks, and leaves, with raised outlines and centres, pearled all round in single rows, or some parts in double and triple relief. A select variety of fancy stitches is introduced in the flowers; the stalks are in solid work, and the ornamental edge forms part of the Lace (illustration No. 17). The whole fabric has a rich and gorgeous effect, especially if executed in coloured or shaded silk. The specimen illustrated on Plate 8, Fig 16, is done in yellow silk; other favourite colours were purple and cream. This costly Point found ready purchasers in the high dignitaries of the Roman priesthood for chasubles, stoles, maniples, corporal cloths, and pall: the laity had to content themselves with collarettes,

FIG. 17. VENETIAN RAISED POINT (late Renaissance Style).

berthes, and laced bands, or cravats. The graduations in degree and extent of raising are infinite, and follow closely the requirements of style and fashion. During the Renaissance period designs in general, and raised parts in particular, were bold and highly ornamental. With the approach of the Rococo period the pattern becomes more disconnected, the relief work lower and scarcer, until only a flat patternless guipure remains of all the glories of Venetian Lacework.

According to Zedler, an author who wrote about Lace in 1744, the price of Venice Point in high relief varied from one to nine ducati per brazza (Italian ell); Venice Point in part relief fetched from four and a half to eight lire the same length.

Lace dealers sometimes call raised Venetian or Spanish Lace *bone point*, from its general aspect of carved ivory; but in olden times bone point meant lace made on the pillow, with sheep bones as bobbins, or fish bones as pins.

Equally misapplied is the term "Caterpillar Point," which is given to a special kind of raised point, in which some of the raised outlines are worked as a row of disks; whereas it refers more generally to Laces in which the fillings bear a resemblance to leaves perforated by caterpillars.

SUBDIVISION B.

PUNTO IN ARIA.

(FLAT POINT.)

This kind of Venetian Point is executed in the same style and manner as Rose Point, the raised parts being omitted. Charming specimens *à bride* of Renaissance work are met with. Towards the close of the seventeenth century, however, Venice was able no longer to compete with the elaborate and costly Points de France, introduced by Colbert 1665, and patronised by Louis XIV. Venice Points were excluded from the mart of fashion by prohibitory edicts, and degenerated into the well-known patternless guipures resembling Irish crochet work. These late Guipures de **Venise are** characterised by the formation of the stalks, which are no longer executed **in solid** work, but in a kind of needle-made braid. These gradually died away, leaving the field to the vigorous offsprings of Venetian teaching—Alençon, Argentan, **or Brussels** Point.

A last effort in artistic Lace, attempted by a few isolated Lace-workers of the **old** Venetian school, was a grounded Point of beautiful workmanship called *Argentella* **or** *Point de Venise à Réseau* (Plate 8, Fig. 15). Made at the beginning of the eighteenth century to compete with Brussels Flat Point, it revived all the old traditions and the consummate skill of former days, and surpasses all contemporary points in beauty of design, fineness of the thread employed, and minuteness of execution. Argentella can be distinguished from a similar Point made at Brussels by the little raised knots scattered over the pattern, and the lozenge shaped devices introduced into the fillings as rows or stars (illustration No. 17). The island of Burano, near Venice, seems to have been the principal centre for Argentella : this kind of Point continued to be made there, although in much inferior workmanship, until the end of last century. In the latest specimens of Burano Point, the ground is a heavy fabric formed of square meshes, the pattern is worked right across the parallel rows, the cordonet left in an unfinished state as a strand of threads, and not overcast with buttonhole stitch.

CHAPTER IX.

SPANISH POINT.

PANISH POINT GUIPURE À BRIDE is altogether different from the so-called *Point d'Espagne*, described in Chapter VII. as a Plaited Pillow Lace executed in gold or silver wire. The real Spanish Point work—raised and flat —closely resembles Venetian Point; but real brides, profusely ornamented and pearled, are substituted for the irregular brided net-ground (illustration No. 18). Favourite appendages of the brides are the pearled coxcomb and star-shaped devices. The impulse to this sumptuous Lacework seems to have been given first through the Moorish embroideries, for which the Spanish Arabs occupying the kingdoms of Valencia, Murcia, and Andalusia, during the Middle Ages, were famous, and then through the school of embroidery established by Philip II. in the convent of the Escorial towards the end of the sixteenth century, and flourishing after the expulsion of the Moriscos in 1610, where exquisite needlework was wrought under the direction of Fray Lorenzo di Monserrate and Diego Rutimer, after the designs of Tibaldi and other great painters. The influence of this school explains the superiority of design in Point Laces of Spanish origin. The scrollwork of ornamented *fleur de lys*, acanthus leaves, and connecting stalks shows far more graceful and easier lines than may be observed in Venetian Point. This work was restricted to a few nunneries, and practised there almost exclusively for the adornment of the innumerable churches, saints, and priests, but very little used for profane dress, as contemporary portraits show. Admirable specimens of this gorgeous Point are preserved in the cathedral of Toledo, where a complete set of vestments and altar fronts, richly embroidered and trimmed with Lace, exists for every one of the principal feasts of the year. The sacristies of the cathedrals at Seville, Granada, Burgos, Segovia, and other Spanish towns, are likewise rich in exquisite textile fabrics, embroideries, and gold, silver, silk, and thread Laces. Hardly anything was known about the sumptuous Raised Point of Spain, beside some pieces "appropriated" by French officers during the Napoleonic invasion, until the sequestration of the monasteries in 1830. The hoarded church Laces were then thrown on the world, to be converted into the manifold appendages of modern dress. Magnificent vestments, altar covers, and frontals appeared in the market, but attracted scanty attention at first. It is only a few years back that the mania for Rose Point set in, and prices are now paid for the same which would astonish even the nuns who stitched it, and little thought their beloved saints would be stripped for worldly women's adornment.

The real Spanish Points seem to have been worked for a comparatively short period in the seventeenth century. The specimens extant are all à bride, and in the purest Renaissance style of bold and large design. No grounded point of Spanish origin is ever met with. There are, of course, gradations with regard to finish of design, but even the coarser pieces are of superior workmanship. A beautiful specimen of Spanish Raised Point is exhibited at the South Kensington Museum, it consists of chasuble, stole, and maniple, with a corporal or small square to place the sacramental cup upon. Nothing can surpass this priceless Lace in beauty of design, marvellous workmanship, and matchless preservation ; and the cost, £200, for which the treasure was purchased from Mr. Blackburn must be considered as very moderate.

Scarcely any other old Point has been so frequently imitated as Spanish Raised Point. The flowers and stalks were either formed with tape or braid, or cut out from solid linen, the outlines buttonholed, and the raised parts sewn on. These imitations are a mockery of the old work, and are valueless.

Sometimes pieces occur more or less skilfully made up of detached flowers and stalks ; they are most valuable to the collector, as they frequently contain fragments of point work made at different periods, and in localities widely apart.

Flat Spanish Point has the appearance of unfinished Raised Point, with the relief work omitted (illustration No. 19). The design looks straggling and monotonous, lacking, as it does, gracefully rounded outlines. Specimens are scarce, and evidently belong to a period when Point Lacemaking in Spain was on the decline.

Portugese Point is identical in design and workmanship with the productions of the sister kingdom.

Point Lace imitating the Spanish style of pattern was made in Italy, and *vice versâ* in Spain, but without affecting to any degree the general character of the Lacework of either country.

The information to be gathered from Spanish authors about Lace in general, and the Raised Point in particular, is, on the whole, very scanty ; but many curious and interesting facts might no doubt be brought to light by a connoisseur who had an opportunity to examine the church treasures in the old Spanish towns.

CHAPTER X.

FRENCH POINT LACE.

HE manufacture of Point Lace in France was established by Colbert (Ordinance dated August 5, 1665) under singular circumstances. All through the first half of the seventeenth century the French kings had endeavoured to put down the extravagant taste of their courtiers and *grandes dames* by sumptuary edicts, regulating dress and fashion. "Lettres patentes pour la réformation du luxe des habits," "Déclarations contre le luxe," were issued again and again, of course wholly in vain—in fact, with the opposite effect. The French nobles *would* lavish their substance in the purchase of the costly Laces of Venice, Genoa, and Flanders, and persisted in squandering thousands of livres for their *rabats, manchettes,* and *canons.* The most stringent ordinance published under Louis XIV., November 27, 1660, prohibiting all foreign points, and even French Laces exceeding an inch in width, was simply laughed at; whereupon Colbert bethought himself of the shrewd expedient of draining the purses of his countrymen into his own exchequer; he set to work to have the coveted Venetian and Spanish points produced in France, and he succeeded well in his effort. Under Colbert's auspices Mme. Gilbert, a native of Alençon procured thirty Italian Laceworkers from Venice, and started the manufacture of Point Lace work at Colbert's Château de Lonray, near Alençon. By the edict mentioned above the establishment was made over to a company, with an exclusive privilege for ten years, and a money grant of 36,000 francs. The plan succeeded admirably, and yielded profits amounting to fifty per cent. upon each share, after the enterprise had been at work only for a few years (1669). A second royal Lace manufactory was set up at the Château de Madrid, in the Bois de Boulogne; and after the lapse of the privilege for Château Lonray, the town of Alençon continued the production with the Point Laceworkers trained by Mme. Gilbert. From Alençon Point Lace-making spread to Argentan, and we cannot do better than describe French Point Lace in three groups: *Point de France, Point d'Alençon, Point d'Argentan.*

POINT DE FRANCE.

(GRAND POINT DE FRANCE BRODÉ À L'ANTIQUE. DENTELLE VOLANTE.)

We limit the term Point de France to the Raised Guipures à Bride made between 1665 and 1720, and apply the special appellations Alençon and Argentan Point to the grounded Laces introduced after 1720. The early Points de France made at Lonray were a close imitation of Raised Venetian and Spanish Points as far as workmanship was concerned; but the design appears considerably improved, with the Spanish style

G 2

for basis. The pattern as a whole shows less stiff and more easily flowing lines. Fleur
de lys and rigid stalks are more or less discarded for a graceful scrollwork of acanthus
leaves, terminating and interspersed with star and rose-shaped flowers. The relief
ornamentation of the raised work was even richer and more elaborate, than in Spanish
Points; so were the brides.

Every kind of Raised Venetian and Spanish Point—with and without brides, with
"brides claires" and "brides ornées"—was successfully copied; but no Flat Point seems
to have been made in France. Pillow Laces of elaborate workmanship took the place of
the latter. Colbert's exertions, it may be here observed, did not stop at needle
Points only; but they likewise extended to the establishment of centres for Pillow Lace-
making at Du Quesnoy, Arras, Rheims, Sedan, Château Thierry, Loudun, and other places,
with the object of competing with the Laces of Genoa and Flanders. All these Laces
were officially called Points de France, and the needle-made Points distinguished by the
designation "Point à l'Aiguille," until Alençon and Argentan (becoming sufficiently known
to the mercantile world as the centres for needle-made Laces) attached their own names
to these productions.

Ordinances and the personal partiality of the Great Monarch went a long way to
exclude all foreign Laces from the French markets; but, on the other side, it must be
acknowledged the Points de France stood on their own merits; they were superior
in design and workmanship to the Venetian and Spanish Points, and well deserved the
patronage so lavishly, bestowed on them throughout the reign of Louis XIV., and long
afterwards. Every article in dress and wear in church, camp, and house was trimmed
with Point de France; altar cloths and church vestments, as well as skirts, mantles,
aprons, gloves, fans, corsets, shirts, towels, shoes, "équipages de lit et de bain," cravats,
ruffles, and manchettes. The quantity of Lace produced by the royal factories during
the second half of the seventeenth century must have been enormous; but still it fell far
short of the immense demand. Although Genoa and Venice were rigorously excluded
from French markets, Flemish Laces to the value of more than £300,000 were imported
into France in 1681. The comparative scarcity of these famous Points at the present
day is, therefore, difficult to explain. Neglected and thrust aside during the Rococo
period, many fine pieces must have perished during the French revolution and the
subsequent decades of strife and indifference.

The same Points which royalty now covets were thrown away as so many rags;
and the writer can well remember the time when Laces of this kind could be bought
for a few shillings, but which are now worth double their weight in gold. There is,
however, every reason to believe that many parures of Point de France still exist in
England, in forgotten places in the mansions of the rich; and it is hoped, that these
Lace treasures will be rescued from decay, not allowed to perish unseen.

In the foregoing remarks we have had in view the Grand Point de France brodé
à l'antique (illustration No. 21), bold in design, and perfect in workmanship, as made
during the lifetime of Louis XIV., and depicted in numberless portraits of his courtiers.
We have now to describe the gradual change to the grounded Points of the eighteenth
century.

The decline of Lace-making in France began under the Regency and Louis XV.

Plate 9.

Fig. 18. SPANISH ROSE POINT (finest Renaissance Style).

FIG. 19. SPANISH FLAT POINT (Renaissance Style).

The picturesque dress, so well adapted to the display of heavy Points, gave way to the stiff and formal attire of the Rococo period; flimsier Lacework was needed for jabots and ruffles. Valenciennes and Brussels Pillow Laces, exquisite in design and workmanship, made formidable competition against the royal Points de France : the latter had to bow to the edicts of fashion and adopt the contracted pattern of the day. The specimens of this period are still à *bride* and with raised centres, but the body of the pattern shrinks to mere buttonholed outlines; yet even these brided skeletons could not find favour, and were abandoned for the grounded points of Alençon and Argentan.

ALENÇON POINT.

(POINT À L'AIGUILLE. POINT D'ALENÇON À RÉSEAU.)

Early in the eighteenth century Brussels seems to have introduced a method of producing grounded Points with greater speed and less cost. This end was attained by subdivision of labour, by assigning to different hands the manifold parts of the Lacework. The Lace manufacturers of Alençon and Argentan adopted this plan, and went even further in the subdivision of labour. If Brussels employed seventeen hands to finish a piece of Lace, Alençon set to work eighteen, each of them trained to one special process. The pattern was printed from a copper plate upon numbered strips of white or green parchment, in sections about ten inches long, and then tacked to a piece of linen folded double. The mounted design now passed through the hands of eighteen women, each of whom was trained from early youth to one special part of the work.

The "piqueuse" had to prick the holes through parchment and linen for the "traceuse," who traced the outline of the pattern with two threads fixed at narrow intervals with minute stitches.

The "réseleuse" and "fondeuse" put in the réseau proper and any other meshwork required.

The "remplisseuse" filled in the flat or toilé of the pattern with close point stitches ; and the surrounding Cordonet or brode was finished by the "brodeuse."

The "modeuse" made the ornamental fillings or buttonholed modes.

"Ebouleuse" and "régaleuse" had to prepare the sections of the pattern for assemblage by cutting the same from the parchment, and arranging them together on a piece of green paper, mounted on double-folded linen of the size and shape ultimately required.

The "assembleuse" then had the difficult and delicate task of joining all the pieces, either by an invisible seam or by the "point de raccroc :" both operations are difficult to describe, but are still practised by experienced French Lace-menders for repairing antique Lace. Four more hands—"toucheuse," "brideuse," "boucleuse," and "gazeuse"—were employed to finish the work of the "assembleuse" before it was handed over to the "mignonneuse," who sewed the engrêlure on and passed it to the "picoteuse," who added the picots to the Cordonet of edge and fillings, keeping the points straight by passing a fine horsehair through the top loops. This horsehair is a peculiarity of the Alençon picots, only found in rare cases in Brussels Needlepoint ; and in many old specimens it is lost, being either purposely or accidentally drawn out. After a piece of

Alençon Point had been finished so far, the "affineuse" completed and amended any minor defects in the working, and handed it over to the "affiqueuse," who removed inequalities in the toilé (inside the Cordonet) by polishing the surface of the flowers with an instrument called "afficot," made of steel, ivory, or hard wood: teeth of animals or lobster claws were used for the same purpose.

The real Alençon ground was of a peculiar make, altogether different from the open buttonhole stitch of the Brussels Point Net; it was worked in straight rows, joined at both ends to the threads used for tracing the pattern, and indicated on the parchment by parallel leading lines, drawn at equal distances of about half an inch apart; its meshes were formed with two threads bound together with a third thread, as an examination with the magnifying glass will show; it was stronger and much more durable than Brussels net, and did not shrink out of shape when washed: for this reason Alençon Point is generally found in better condition than Brussels of equal age, although the latter is easier to repair. The patterns of Alençon belong all either to the Rococo (illustration No. 22), or to the dotted style (illustration No. 20), and are inferior to those used for Argentan Point. Specimens with figures—generally saints—coats of arms or devices occur; but these are rare.

Alençon seems to have been the favourite Point for demi-toilette, and only narrow border Laces, and shaped pieces, as lappets, caps, &c., were produced; neither flounces nor parures were made. Alençon could not compete even in workmanship with similar Laces made at Argentan and Brussels; the fillings, especially, were neither so elaborate nor so varied.

In prosperous times the Lace district of Alençon extended over a radius of four miles round the town, and gave employment to 9000 hands, producing Laces to the value of 1,200,000 livres; but the manufacture declined gradually towards the latter end of the eighteenth century, and experienced only a short revival under Napoleon I., the Emperor having had some large orders in Alençon Point, on pillow-made ground, executed for the Empress Marie Louise, and for the King of Rome. The mode of making the true Alençon ground, which defies time and wear, remains lost and forgotten: and modern attempts to rescue this art from oblivion have signally failed. Although Alençon still produces Point Lace, the flowers are all appliqué to machine-made net, and the entire fabric partakes of the flimsy character of modern Laces. A few "corbeilles de mariage" and consequent layettes for imperial and royal use cannot sustain an art-industry in times of chronic decrease of emperors and kings; and the general public will not or cannot pay the prices artistic Lacework must necessarily command.

The finest modern Alençon Point is made at Bayeux, in the factory of Mr. A. Lefébure: this manufacturer exhibited in 1867 a magnificent dress, valued at 80,000f.

ARGENTAN POINT.

The date when Point Lacemaking was first taken up at Argentan is uncertain. The name of the place is not mentioned in Colbert's edicts; and it occurs in public records only after 1800; but there can be hardly any doubt, that braided Points de France were made at Argentan prior to 1700. Very likely a small colony of Laceworkers, inmates

Plate 10.

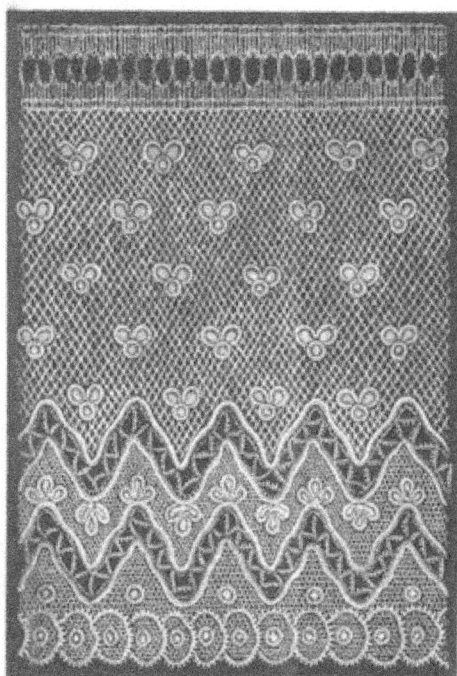

Fig. 20. Alençon Point (Dotted Style).

Fig. 21. Point de France (Louis XIV. Period).

of the hospital of St. Louis, worked for the royal fabrics from the very beginning of the latter; but the quantity produced was too insignificant to bring the locality of origin prominently forward; or perhaps the Laceworkers of Argentan were prevented by the privileges granted to the royal manufacturers to trade under their own name. However that may be, the Point Lace made at Argentan must always have been of a high class, superior in workmanship and design to Alençon Point, and so it remained all through the eighteenth century. The mode of working was much the same as described under Alençon; but the design was bolder, and the fillings retained the character of the Venetian school with regard to minute workmanship, careful execution, and variety of ornamental stitches. The *characteristic* feature in Argentan Point is the clear and well-defined ground called "bride," and consisting of hexagonal meshes, each side worked over with minute buttonhole stitches. The ground was fully printed on the parchment pattern, and the six corners were secured with pins to obtain regularity of the

Fig. 22. Alençon Point (Rococo Style).

hexagon. When used for fillings picots were added to the buttonholed sides of the mesh (bride picotée, bouclée, or épinglée), a device frequently found in Brussels Needle Point. The grounded Points of Argentan all belong to the Rococo (illustration No. 23) and dotted style (illustration No. 24), but are designed in much better taste than contemporary Alençon Laces. Argentan and Brussels may be considered as the prominent Points of the eighteenth century; they were used not only for borderings and minor articles of wear, but for flounces, parures, and garnitures, worn by dignitaries of the Church, the nobility, and the well-to-do classes on festive occasions.

The extent of the Argentan fabric was limited to three or four establishments, and the number of Lace-workers connected with the manufacture seems not to have exceeded 2000 at any time. Very remunerative orders only were executed, and slop-work was thus avoided.

H

Mrs. Palliser, in her "History of Lace," p. 177, gives a curious extract from the accounts of Madame du Barry, relating to the price of Argentan Point.

1772. " Un ajustement de point d'Argentan—
    " Les 6 rangs manchettes.
    " 1/3 pour devant de gorge.
    " 4 au. 1/3 festonné des deux costés, le fichu et une
        garniture de fichu de nuit . . . .   2500 livres.
    " 1 au. 3/4 ruban de point d'Argentan, à 100 . . .   175 —
    " Une collerette de point d'Argentan . . . . . .   360 —
           (*Comptes de Madame du Barry*.)

Frequent attempts were made during the eighteenth century to set up new workshops for Argentan Point, either in the town or in the neighbourhood (at Mortagne and Carrouge) ; but the old-established manufacturers—Guyard and Du Ponchet, in connection with the Hospital of St. Louis—seem to have jealously guarded their royal prerogative, and influenced the authorities to refuse further licenses for that purpose. Argentan Point remained a Lace for the highest classes of society, difficult to obtain, and of great value. Tasteful designs and careful workmanship were kept up by the privileged factories until the storms of the Revolution put an end to a manufacture altogether, which has never been, and probably never will be, revived. For this reason, as well as for the real beauty of the work, the scarce remnants of it ought to be carefully preserved and collected, even in preference to the "Point de France" and "Point d'Alençon," both of which are much more likely to be successfully imitated. Amongst the Lace specimens, exhibited at the South Kensington Museum, is a magnificent flounce of Point d'Argentan ; but, being unfortunately placed near to the ceiling of a dark corner, it is often overlooked by visitors.

Plate 11.

FIG. 23. ARGENTAN POINT (early Rococo Style).

FIG. 24. ARGENTAN POINT (late Rococo Style).

CHAPTER XI.

BRUSSELS POINT.

[POINT DE BRUXELLES À L'AIGUILLE; POINT D'ANGLETERRE À L'AIGUILLE.]

HE Lace generally known under the name of Brussels Point is not real Point, but is made on the pillow. "Point plat" (as it is called in Belgium) formed at all times the great feature of the Brussels Lace manufacture; "Point de Bruxelles à l'Aiguille," although far superior in workmanship, was decidedly inferior in commercial importance. In this chapter we have only to consider the needle-wrought Lace, and defer the far-famed productions of the Brussels pillow to a future chapter.

FIG. 25. SPRIG OF BRUSSELS NEEDLE POINT (late Renaissance Style).

We cannot find any traces of needle-made point guipures à bride which could be with any likelihood ascribed to Brussels manufacture. The working of real Point seems only to have been taken up there at the beginning of the eighteenth century, when grounded Points became the fashion. These early Points were merely imitations of "Point de Venise à Réseau," of Alençon and Argentan Point, and so much resemble the models they are copied from that they can only be distinguished by the ground, which differs from the Argentan brided net as well as from the Alençon Réseau. Brussels Point Lace Réseau is a simple needle-made ground, done in open buttonhole stitch (see Diagrams.). Its character and mode of working have not been altered to the present day. It is now made on the bobbin-net machine introduced into Belgium by Mr. Washer in 1834, and it is used as ground for the pillow flowers of Brussels and other application Laces.

BRUSSELS NEEDLE-MADE GROUND.

Minor peculiarities of Brussels Needle Point are the finer and somewhat more open (grillé) point stitch work in which the flowers are executed ; the absence or scarcity of picots along the outlines of the pattern, the pearls being generally confined to the edge, is another characteristic.

Old Venetian Laces seem to have been taken as models for filling up the "modes," and the superiority of this arrangement and workmanship was universally acknowledged at the time. It is even reported that Alençon and Argentan Points were sent to Brussels to be finished by putting in the ornamental stitches.

The earliest Brussels Needle Point was made towards the end of the Renaissance period. It closely resembles the grounded point of Venice in workmanship, but essentially differs from it in design, and never shows the small raised knobs in the pattern characteristic of the former. The sprig (illustration No. 25) is a fine example of the flower and leafage pattern so frequently met with in Brussels Point and Pillow Laces, and rarely ever found in Laces of Italian origin. The flimsy pearled brides in the fillings likewise indicate the Flemish origin of this specimen.

To the same period belongs the crown of an infant's cap, figured in illustration No. 26. From Queen Elizabeth's time the christening suit—shirt, cap, and "bearing cloth"—given to a child by its sponsors was trimmed with Lace. Cutwork and Reticella of the finest kind were used during the seventeenth century, and a suit of this description, exquisitely worked, is exhibited at the South Kensington Museum. Later, fine point insertions made at Brussels, with an openwork pattern representing the Tree of Knowledge, the Flower-pot of the Annunciation, and the Holy Dove, came into fashion.

Brussels Point during the eighteenth century follows, like Alençon and Argentan, the Rococo and dotted style in design, but retains the elaborate character in its "jours," as shown in illustration No. 27, until it shrinks, under the influence of the First Empire to mere outline work (illustration No 28).

After the French Revolution had destroyed the Lace industry of Alençon and Argentan, Brussels stood alone in the manufacture of costly Points ; and it remains so to

Plate 12.

Fig. 26. CROWN OF A CHRISTENING CAP IN BRUSSELS POINT (Eighteenth Century).

FIG. 27. BRUSSELS NEEDLE POINT (Rococo Style).

the present day. Napoleon I. was a great lover of Lace, and patronised the Brussels fabric by large orders for the Empress Maria Louise, the King of Rome, and the Pope; but the old French nobility, at all times the chief patrons of fine Laces, had lost the means for luxury and extravagance, and the manufacture of the finer needle points was for many years very limited after the downfall of Napoleon. A certain deterioration with regard to workmanship was the necessary consequence. Besides, in 1818, the bobbin-net machine was universally adopted for making the net ground; and twenty years after the Jacquard cards were applied to weave the pattern. Europe now became inundated with cheap machine-made Laces; and Brussels, not to be driven entirely from the markets, had to cheapen her manufactures and reserve her finer Lacework for special orders. Under these circumstances it must be considered as most creditable to the Brussels Lace manufacturers not to have given up the production of Point Lace altogether. However, the International Exhibitions (commencing 1851), and a period of financial prosperity, gave a new stimulus to the trade in finer Laces; and since then Brussels has steadily improved her points in design as well as in workmanship.

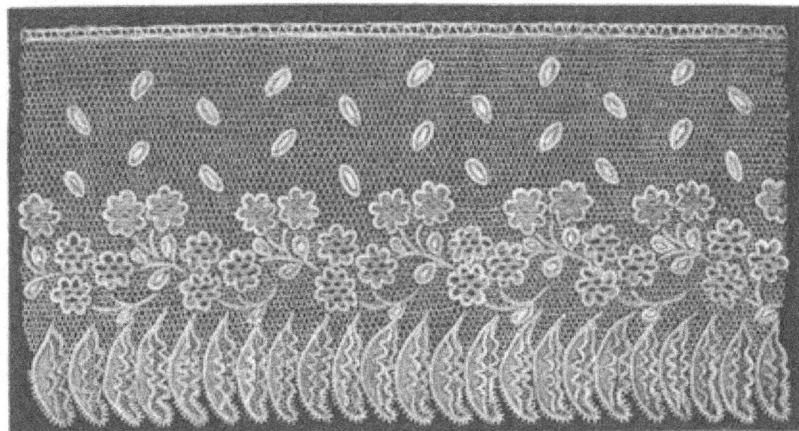

Fig. 28.   Brussels Needle Point (Dotted style).

At the present time two kinds of Needle Point, distinguished by different names, are made at Brussels—*Point Gaze, Point à l'Aiguille Appliqué.*

POINT GAZE.

The *Point Gaze* (No. 29) is made in small pieces, flowers and ground (vraie réseau) simultaneously, entirely by hand; the sections are afterwards joined along a vertical outline of the pattern. The Cordonet consists of a group of threads, not over-cast with buttonhole stitch, as in the antique fabric, but fixed to the outlines by a continuous

I

row of stitches. This arrangement distinguishes old from modern Brussels Point. The flowers are executed in plain clothing and Brussels stitches, part of the leaves in close tissue—the other part more open, and embroidered with minute dots. This variety produces a pleasing effect of shading, and brings out the relief work of the pattern. The "jours" are filled in with embroidered wheel and star devices, and the "picots" are executed as simple loops.

Point Gaze passes through three hands: the "gazeuse" makes the flowers and the réseau; the "brodeuse" places and fixes the Cordonet for the relief work; the "fonneuse" works the fancy stiches for the "jours." These three hands will finish a yard of *Point Gaze*, medium quality and two inches wide, in three to four weeks, and will earn from 1fr. 25c. to 3fr. 50c. per day. The thread used for modern Brussels Point is spun at Ghent, and varies in price from 50fr. to 1500fr. per lb., according to fineness.

POINT À L'AIGUILLE APPLIQUÉ.

The needle-made flowers and leafage of this Point are worked separately in the same style and manner as Point Gaze patterns, but afterwards appliqué on, or, to use a more correct expression, inserted into Washer's machine-made tulle or Brussels net. The net is cut away underneath the pattern: this device gives the Lace the appearance of continuity, and avoids the patchy character of thorough appliqué work.

The pillow-made Laces of modern Brussels manufacture, called Point de Médici, Point Duchesse (or Point de Flandre), Point de Paris, Point de Venice (flat flowers with needle-made ground), and Plat Appliqué, we shall describe in their proper place under Brussels Pillow Lace.

For the original of the lappet engraved on Plate 13, and for valuable information concerning the modern Brussels Lacework, we are indebted to Messrs. Buchholtz and Co., 1, Rue Leopold, Bruxelles, one of the leading Lace manufacturers in Belgium. This firm employs 5000 to 6000 hands, and has branch establishments in nearly every capital of Europe—London, Paris, Vienna, Milan, St. Petersburgh, Moscow. Part of their workpeople are living in Brussels; but the greater number are scattered all over Belgium, in the Lace districts of South Brabant, Antwerp, West Flanders, and East Flanders.

At the Vienna Exhibition Messrs. Buchholtz and Co. obtained the first prize of merit for a complete garniture in *Point Gaze* with raised flowers in floating relief, consisting of a large half shawl; 7yds. flouncing, 18in. wide; 7yds. flouncing, 8in. wide; a berthe measuring 6yds., and 4½in. wide; lappet, parasol cover, fan, and handkerchief; value, 40,000fr. It took twelve of the most experienced Laceworkers three years to produce this garniture, which certainly was one of the sights at the great industrial gathering, and worthily represented the ancient glories of Brussels Lacework.

Plate 13.

Fig. 29. BRUSSELS POINT GAZE (Modern).

CHAPTER XII.

ENGLISH POINT.

HETHER Needle Point proper has at any time been manufactured on a large scale in England, is dubious. Some writers assert that a kind of Point Guipure, in the style of early Point de France, was made at Blandford in Dorsetshire, to the value of £30 a yard; and in the Proceedings of the Anti-Gallican Society it is recorded that a prize for Needle Point ruffles was awarded to a Mrs. Elizabeth Waterman, of Salisbury, in 1751. We never have been able to find an authenticated specimen of this Blandford Point, and have reason to believe that it was a Pillow-made Lace of elaborate workmanship. Certain it is that English ladies excelled in imitations of some leading Points of the seventeenth and eighteenth centuries; but this work is all more or less of the Reticella type, the patterns of the later specimens slightly influenced by the Renaissance style (illustration No. 29). The thread employed differs from that used for Italian and Flemish Laces in substance, colour, and touch; and the characteristic feature of this English Point is a quaint homely pattern, which leaves no doubt about its origin. Specimens are very rarely met with, although old sets of great beauty exist as heirlooms in old English families. The best and most artistic patterns for English Point Lace are given in "*The Needle's Excellency, a new booke, wherein are divers admirable workes wrought with the needle, newly invented and cut in copper for the pleasure and profit of the industrious.* 1640." This interesting pattern book, oblong 4to., contains more than a hundred beautiful patterns for Lace, needlework, and embroidery. It is the only work of this kind published in England at so early a date; and the text "in prayse of the needle" is written by John Taylor, the Water Poet, in verse. Strange to say, there is no copy of this book either in the British Museum or in the Art Library at South Kensington.

Most curious and clever imitations of Alençon and Brussels Point in Rococo style are sometimes met with; the flowers are cut out of linen, the Cordonet is formed in rope-stitch with a thick thread, and the ground is put in with the needle. These specimens are very deceptive even at a short distance, but of course are instantly recognisable as counterfeits on closer examination.

It would be interesting to ascertain the time when Irish crochet work and the so-called Irish Point were first made. The patterns being evidently taken from Spanish Guipures and early "Point de France," no doubt this needlework could be traced back to the beginning of the eighteenth century, if not to an earlier period.

Of late the Irish Laceworkers have taken to reproduce the heavy point guipures of the seventeenth century, and very creditable work of this kind with regard to pattern has come into the market. Unfortunately, the thread is coarse, woolly, of a bad colour, and very indifferently spun. A finer and whiter thread would materially improve the hand-made modern Point Lacework; and all these Laces ought to be submitted to a process of singeing—"gasing," as the Nottingham Lace manufacturers call it—which burns off the loose fibres without any injury to the work.

The needle-made Laces mentioned and described in the preceding chapters are the only recognised real Points. Isolated Point Lace-workers were found in many countries—in Germany, Holland, Switzerland, Denmark, and Sweden—especially

Fig. 30. English Point (late Seventeenth Century)

after the Edict of Nantes, which scattered the cleverest French workpeople all over Europe. But these individual efforts scarcely left any trace in the commercial world, and the name "Point" applied to Laces, made in these countries, relates in nearly every instance to productions of the pillow. Lace collectors should bear this fact well in mind, so as not to be deceived if some uncommon-looking Lace be offered to them under a high-sounding, fancy name.

END OF THE SECOND DIVISION.

VALUE OF POINT LACE.

With regard to the relative value in England, the different Point Laces rank as follows:

1. Spanish and Italian Raised Points and early **Point de France.**
2. Spanish and Italian Flat Points.
3. Argentan.
4. Brussels Needle Point.
5. Alençon.

And the following scale of prices for pieces of a good serviceable length and shape, in perfect condition, will be found generally correct.

Spanish and Italian Raised Points and early Points de France are worth 30s. to 40s. per yard, and one inch width.
Spanish and Italian Flat Points, from 25s. to 30s. the same length and width.
Argentan, Brussels, and Alençon, from 15s. to 25s. per yard, and one inch width.

Of course, pieces of exceptional beauty as regards design and workmanship, and of rare preservation, fetch exceptional and comparatively much higher prices.

ARRANGEMENT OF LACE SPECIMENS IN A **COLLECTION.**

Lace, like other collections, requires thought and consideration in arranging. The fashion, which is now so general, of collecting specimens of lace is only a revival, with this difference, that whereas in old days ladies amassed long lengths and large quantities, now they are content with scraps of small dimensions. Formerly Lace collections were hidden in presses and cabinets, now they are for public inspection; and the general idea is to arrange them in albums, as drawing-room table ornaments.

A few suggestions, from experience, how to show Lace specimens to the best advantage **may** therefore be **of** interest.

The desirable length of Lace specimens for a collection is regulated by the pattern, the whole of **which** ought to be shown. Eight inches are, with very few exceptions, sufficient for **this** purpose; **in** many cases four or six inches. The specimens can be mounted on silk **or** canvas, cloth, or velvet; but black glazed paper of good quality answers by far the best, and shows both workmanship and design to the greatest advantage. Silk and canvas grease and discolour; cloth and velvet retain the dust.

The specimen to be mounted is first of all properly stretched and trimmed, and then tacked on a piece of black glazed paper of suitable size, with stitches short in front, and about one inch apart at the back. Too many tacking stitches ruffle Lace and paper ; a little practice will teach how to tack a piece of Lace evenly and smoothly on to paper. The edges of the paper are then cut, not with scissors, but with a sharp penknife and rule on a plane of soft wood or stout cardboard, leaving a margin round the Lace about one quarter of an inch wide.

The specimen so mounted is gummed to a second piece of glazed paper—blue for Point Lace, red for Pillow Lace—overreaching the mount one quarter to one half of an inch. Gumming at the corners and at a few points between is quite sufficient, and preferable to entire pasting down. Care should be taken to use the gum not too fluid, but rather sticky. The specimen is now ready to be put in an album.

The handiest size for a Lace album is 12in. by 9¼in. quarto. Specimens of 8in. length and under find space across one page ; specimens from 8in. to 16in. can be put in lengthwise or across two pages.

In an album of double the size given above specimens 16in. long can be arranged across one page, the shorter scraps in two rows.

The album should contain leaves of smooth and moderately stiff mounting board of a grey tint—white being objectionable for showing dust stains—the leaves should be separated by guards to prevent bulging when the album is full. The pressure of the leaves on the Lace keeps the latter straight and smooth without injury ; all precautions besides the guards to keep the leaves asunder are therefore unnecessary.

The number of guards between the leaves depends on the thickness of the mounted specimens. For Mediæval Lacework, Raised Points, and heavy Pillow Laces, four guards ; for Flat Points and fine Pillow Laces two guards will be found sufficient.

The mounted specimens are gummed to the right-hand page of the album ; the left-hand page is used for manuscript remarks, engravings, woodcuts, and photographs relating to Lace. The specimens on their mounts can be framed in with lines in gold, Indian or coloured ink, or with ornamental borders ; but the plain plan will always show best. The specimens so disposed can easily be removed and transferred to another page by passing a paper-knife under the mount.

Three sets of albums are desirable for a Lace collection—one for Mediæval Lacework, one for Point Lace, one for Pillow Lace. Mediæval Lacework is best arranged in sections relating to workmanship and style of pattern ; Point and Pillow Lace according to country of origin, subdivided into chronological periods of style.

The outside ornamentation of the album must be left to the taste of the collector, but different colours should be chosen for the covers of the three sets.

www.ingramcontent.com/pod-product-compliance
Lightning Source LLC
Chambersburg PA
CBHW021531270326
41930CB00008B/1191